RED LETTER DAYS

RED LETTER DAYS

By
MOLLY KEANE
AND SNAFFLES

*With eight illustrations in colour
and a new preface by*
MOLLY KEANE

ANDRE DEUTSCH

This edition first published October 1987 by
André Deutsch Limited
105-106 Great Russell Street
London WC1B 3LJ

Second impression December 1987

Originally published by Collins in 1933
with the text under the pseudonym "M. J. Farrell"
used at that time by Molly Keane

ISBN 0 233 98159 4

Printed in Great Britain by
St Edmundsbury Press Limited, Bury St Edmunds, Suffolk

PREFACE

When I was a young writer my thoughts and my books were all on foxhunting. It was a way of life and a religion with me, and Snaffles was one of its highest priests.

We were all young then and Snaffles pictures canonised our closest aspirations for ourselves, for the men in our lives, and for the performance of our horses. When we knew that he was coming to County Wexford to stay with George Hudson-Kinahan for a day with the Island Hounds, the pack of which George was then Master, our excitement was boundless. We cherished our best horse for the day when he would be out and gave a lot of thought to our own kit and general turnout. In the event, a wet morning, and a long hack on to the meet rather took the sparkle out of our best efforts.

The hounds met at a lonely crossroads with a white-washed pub at one corner. The first draw, a stony, gorse-grown hill, had the rain beating mercilessly into its dark little heart.

At the meet we sat on our wet horses chattering to each other, dissembling curiosity, when we saw a little man get out of the Master's car and onto one of his best horses.

Snaffles looked a bit uncertain at that moment, rather pale and distant (Hudson-Kinahan's port was notorious). I remember he wore a tobacco-brown covert coat and a blue birds-eye scarf, tied as neat as a stock, but rather avant-garde in those days. He was like a bird, perched up on a big fresh bay horse.

I think this day was to be his first experience of an Irish country and he may well have felt a little apprehensive. Galway Blazers, Limerick, Scarteen, Meath, were all to follow this venture with the Island.

Apprehensive or not, he was always there, or thereabouts, in the moderately good hunt we had later in the day. I really cannot remember proper details of that hunt; only that there was no wire on the stone-faced banks and no tarmac on the roads we jumped into and out of. How hounds accounted for their fox is a blank in my mind. What I don't forget is the hack back to the crossroads where the Master's car waited for him and my wet rain-coat waited for me – we rode along together, talking with the ease in which all shyness evaporates after a good hunt. I remember his delighted giggle in the recall of an uncomfortable moment he had survived in the course of the chase. What is still fresh and surprising to me is his amazing power of observation. Most people think of nothing but their own progress or disaster in the course of a hunt, especially so when a stranger in a strange country, but Snaffles had seen and remembered everything. Endless comments must have gone through his mind and he fixed their memories with his questions:

"Who was the old lady who went so well on the grey horse?" . . . .

"The tough, tidy fellow riding a showy sort of chestnut with proper discretion?" . . . .

"The young farmer over-facing his young horse with passionate determination?" . . . .

Some aspect of all he observed was to stay in his mind before it lived on in his capture of the living moment. The vital characteristic is caught unfalteringly in the picture of every horse and every rider he has painted – he gets each peculiarity right, even to the faults in a man's hands or seat; or the big knee on an old and trusted hunter as he comes down off a dreadful hairy bank.

Snaffles had a true and uncritical liking for, and sympathy with, people that prompted the diligence of his observation. He was a kind and gentle man. He was thoughtful too. I don't forget how, on that cold wet evening, before he sought the comforts stored in the boot of the Master's car, he gave me his horse to hold, while he dived into the dark depths of the pub in the corner, and came out with a packet of ginger biscuits and a large Port and Brandy, to shorten my long way home.

"Good Night."

"Good Night . . . ." we said. And I never expected to see him again. Or even dreamed that *Red Letter Days* was to be the outcome of that rather indifferent day with the Island Hounds.

MOLLY KEANE

Snaffles (Charlie Johnson Payne) was born in 1884 and died in 1967. For some fifty years he chronicled sporting, military and naval life, all of which he participated in. Twice he had to leave the army because of ill-health (the Royal Garrison Artillery in 1906 and the Leicestershire Yeomanry, after a year, in 1912). In 1916 he enlisted in the Royal Naval Auxiliary Service, and in 1917 he was commissioned as a Lieutenant in the Royal Naval Volunteer Reserve. He was modest about his work as an artist, regarding its development into a career as a lucky chance. He may have visited Ireland as early as 1908, and certainly did so several times between 1919 and 1933, when *Red Letter Days* was first published. 'One of the finest horse artists of today' (*The Field*) had a hunter of his own for a short time before the First World War, but had after that to rely on borrowed horses, as Molly Keane describes.

TO THE H-K's

With acknowledgments to the *Tatler* and *Illustrated Sporting and Dramatic News*.

CONTENTS

LIST OF COLOUR PLATES

CHAPTER I

A DAY IN COUNTY WEXFORD

WEXFORD is the real paradise for those fox-hunters who want the blood and bones of the thing, those bred to love sport rather than to follow fashion.

A wild sort of country. Hardly a strand of wire. Not a great deal of plough, and what there is rides light. Tarmac nearly unknown. The obstacles? Principally high, narrow banks, faced up with stones. And we don't mind admitting it takes a real good 'un to reach the top of some of these. You don't want a horse that makes fun of his fences. You want him to take them seriously. The brightest equine star in Wexford is an old cock-tailed horse with a big knee and a wise eye. He *loves* jumping. Jumping is his delight, and he'll go and stay. That's the sort you want.

And the coverts? Strong gorse growing in disconnected patches down the length of a bog. Slack drawing hounds are no use here. They must draw the last bush in a covert. So fatally easy it is to draw over a fox lying up on one of those dry secret ledges they love.

"WHERE A CROW CAN GO, HE CAN GO."

Wexford carries for the most part a good holding sort of scent, but with the difficulty of too frequent coverts, you want extra drive to catch a fox. You'd swear, for Wexford, hounds must be much smaller than the Peterboro' standard. A little active hound you need for this enclosed country. How many scores of times in a hunt do hounds have to bore through and creep over a fence, which the little active hound can do while the big lumbering brute will be left in the ditch? Now look at old Warrior, as unlike the Peterboro' type as he well can be, wiry and active, with no pretensions towards beauty. But he looks like galloping, all the same. He goes into the thick stuff too, like a hero. His voice in covert means the real thing— worth a guinea a box, it is—and he'll hunt and catch hold of a fox by himself. . . . But why talk? " All time is surely lost wot is not spent in 'unting."

Were you ever out at a Patrick's Day meet? Well, perhaps not. A typical March hunting day it is. There's a bright sun in the sky and dust blowing up off the plough. No smell—you may swear if you like—but wait.

A mixed gathering of regular members of the hunt and Patrick's Day holiday makers (these last mounted on horses seemingly of two ages only, three, or twenty-three year olds) jog down the single village street as hounds move off to their first draw. There's the Master with a varminty old farmer riding up alongside him full of fox-news. There's a girl with blue eyes and a blue habit, and a very efficient way with her over-fresh cob. An obvious young gunner home on leave, wearing super-extra rat-catcher, is having a rough time with his hireling. And Ireland's first artist in the buying and selling of horseflesh has a keen eye out for a hidden star among the holiday throng.

"Where a crow can go, he can go." A youth on a great

raking, raw-boned chestnut answers an inquiry as to his horse's jumping powers. "And b'God ye'd kill three men gallopin' this horse before ye'd tire him. Well, now," he said a little later after a school over a gap, fenced simply but effectively by the felling across it of a young ash tree, a school in which his mount singularly failed to fulfil that boasted prowess, "this horse'd make a liar o' Saint Paul!"

Knockrobbin bog, the first draw, proves blank, but half a. mile on Swaine's Marlhole (strong-growing gorse on the sunny side of a steep little hill) holds one of the right breed.

"... Yip.... Garn-awii.... Awii.... Aw-*ii*..."

Now how many of us get the right shock of courage that the view of a good fox stealing determinedly out of covert should impart? Slipping across the corner of a field, he doesn't seem to hurry, but for all that he is out of sight in a breath. And the knowledge that the Patrick's Day whisky is still quick in many of his field lends a frenzied liveliness to the doubled notes on the huntsman's horn. He knows how little room his hounds will be given until that spurious courage dies. As well it dies so easy.

A minute's tense wait as his hounds come to him, straining through the strong gorse. Another minute and they are dropping off the fence out of the covert. Old Warrior (in the lead, as always), Actress, Tell-tale, Acrobat, Sampler (best of the young hounds), and fifteen couples more—real stout fox-catchers—have it now.

"Steady, now! Steady. *Please!* For God's sake give hounds a chance——"

Hear old Warrior's deep note and young Sampler throw his tongue in ecstasy as they stoop to the line before they drive out across the first field. God's own most chosen gallantry— a right pack of hounds. Into Knockrobbin again and after a

" This Horse'd make a liar o' Saint Paul ! "

turn round the covert they have their fox away up wind. It's for Ballymore Hill he's pointing, and now the elect of the field show up a bit. The cunning and the cautious know of a better lane.

There's the Master and his Whipper-in right with them; there's that blue girl sending her cob along into a high, narrow one; a young farmer is riding with nice judgment wide on the left of hounds, and behind them the less ambitious of the field —those who would jump any fence, only provided that some one else has had a go at it first—plug along.

A bank with a blind ditch on the landing side, another straight one (this stops a few), a cattle gap in the corner of a field (quick as a knife the blue girl has seen it), and hounds are momentarily checked crossing a narrow lane. Here the young farmer, jumping out before hounds are over the lane, receives a few kind words from the Master. Just as the road contingent casts up old Warrior has it again, over the fence, and hounds are straining up the bracken-grown side of Ballymore Hill. No obstacles, but a bit of a test on wind and fitness, this pull up, and from the top with that " I-wonder-where-I-*will*-take-it " feeling a blown horse gives one, it is a pleasure not quite unmixed with anxiety to see hounds hunting steadily down the farther side. Not such a scent now, but still good enough to hunt a fox.

Over a couple of stone walls and we're with them again, and now on the grass they start to run on and take a bit of staying with. Through Rockspring, where scent (though not the going) improves, they hunt on beautifully into Ballytracey. Never at fault, but they've righted themselves; driving on like wolves over the grass; stooping to it in the dry plough. Now their fox is turning and running short up the ditch sides, but they are never over his line by an inch, turning short with him

THE BRIGHTEST EQUINE STAR IN WEXFORD IS AN OLD COCK-TAILED HORSE WITH A BIG KNEE AND A WISE EYE.

"The old horse looks strong and well, Micky!"

ASKING QUESTIONS OF IT TO WHICH MANY A BETTER HORSE MIGHT HAVE GIVEN
A SILLIER ANSWER.

every time. God send they don't change in Ballytracey bog.

Horses are tiring now. The blue girl is still marvellously here. But she takes hold of her cob and gives him a reminder going into his fences now. So is the young gunner with a very muddy coat and a much subdued hireling. He's had value for his two pounds. And so, strangely enough, is that young horse who so lately made a liar of Saint Paul. Blind banks, high banks and narrow banks, he has dealt with them all somehow. No wonder the world loves a Wexford horse. They learn their job in a hard school and they learn it young.

There's one more enthusiast for the chase present. Fired by a truly divine excitement—a madness for the chase many might envy him—this young lad unyoked his horse from its ploughing and leaving the jennet, its fellow labourer, to follow its own devices, he mounted and pursued the hunt for the last twenty minutes, God knows with what horrible dangers to his person. Speed or skill in leaping his mount has none, but somehow has he caused it to negotiate the obstacles, asking questions of it to which many a better horse might have given a sillier answer. With trousers tucked into his socks, cap back to front, and heart bang in the right place, he deserves remembrance— more power to him !

Short of Ballytracey bog, with a sudden hot sun in the sky, hounds threw up for the first time—a case for a cast. A wild holloa on brings the Master galloping to where an old man with a grey beard flying round his head stands shouting on a fence.

" Did you see the fox ? "

" I did, yer honour, I did ! He come into the covert last night, now it might be ten o'clock, an' his tail up over his back an' he roaring like a lion ! "

For three things is the soul of a huntsman wrung : for a tired fox ; for a failing scent ; for the ways of a fool. But——

" Now *blast* all Women ! "

" There's a couple o' hounds hunting out the end of the bog, Master," said the youth on the plough horse. It was indeed his moment. Fire darting from his eyes, he set about his mount with the slack of the rope reins.

Old Priestess and young Sampler are the couple on, and praying still it may not be a fresh fox, the huntsman puts the rest on to them. Now they're out of the bog and across the road. With the Harrow on their right and Tobergal on their left, they are pointing over the hill towards Knocknaskeogh—right out of the day's draw and unstopped.

" Now *blast* all women ! " he raps out as the blue girl puts her cob at the rotten bank out of the road. Room is all he asks —room for his hounds to hunt. And then, not two fields in front of them, he has a view of a little beaten fox, going stiffly, stiltedly up the side of a fence. God bless old Priestess and Sampler too (best of young hounds). Now see them all drive out along the grass headland of a ploughed field, pour in a toppling wave over the lowest point in a blind fence (not so low but a stiff little fox has nearly fallen back as he topped it) ; a silence and a growling in the ditch.

" *They have him !* "

Which ends a good hunt with the death of a fox—and *every* hound on when they caught him.

CHAPTER II

AN IRISH POINT-TO-POINT

WE passed a horse-box, then three sheeted horses being led from the station to the course. The April sun shone hot on the road, and the road dust blew thick as flour on the bright air. This last long hill saw the end of our journey to the Brackna Hunt point-to-point races.

" Race card ! Race card ! A shillin' the race card," shrilled their purveyors as they leapt on the running-board of our car, wrenched at the door handles, and thrust their heated faces in at the windows. In Ireland nothing accomplishes itself without a grand passion—not even the selling of race cards.

Five shillings for the car—delivered up to an individual hardly more inspiring of confidence than the programme sellers—and we had bumped through a rough gap and parked our car on a hillside where motor-cars, horses, tents, games of chance and skill and bookmakers' stands were inextricably intermingled.

But a good view of the course spread itself below us. Hardly a fence but we must see them jump it, we decided, as our glasses picked up the distant flutter of white flags.

" They want a few more red flags to keep them up to the white ones," somebody suggested, " this is a course that gets a lot of quiet improvement."

" Well, it wants it badly enough " ; here spoke a more indulgent mind, " these banks are too high and too straight, and most of them are leaning towards you. I tell you, you wouldn't like to be riding a tiring horse into some of them.

" THERE'S NOT ONE FENCE ON IT WHERE A MAN WOULD MEET DEATH."

Shall we go and have a look at the horses going out for this open light-weight race? We will!" We went.

Nearly ten minutes later we were still striving towards the paddock. The crowd which seethed around and within its sacred enclosure barred the progress of horses, owners, and jockeys equally with our own. Men, women, and children, they gathered about the saddling. They criticised with able brevity the prowess of the jockeys, the appearance of the horses, and the extreme simplicity of the course.

" There's not one fence on it where a man would meet death," I heard one lady observe in disappointed tones to a friend. And the response: " Wait now till you see how they'll crucify one another in the gaps—that'll be the divil's divarsion."

" Oh, look! Look at Micky," they said, suddenly keyed to tense observation.—" Well, isn't he a lovely fella—and the owld horse looks well too."

Against the ring of far mountains we saw them, against the grave distance and low Irish skies, Micky and the old horse. A likely lad, Micky—a real hardy type. His green satin jacket had seen better days, or nights perhaps, as his sister's party dress. His spurs sloped long and dangerously from the heels of his boots and he was riding a hardy old customer; a big ugly blood horse that looked as if he might gallop and stay for ever, neither the weight nor the going troubling him at all.

" The old horse looks strong and well, Micky "—a silver-haired priest stepped up to the pair of them in the saddling enclosure—" a picture he looks. Fit and big in himself——" The Eye of the Church, bright blue and knowing, dwelt approvingly on the pair of them.

The old priest whispered something one could not hear—

some low spoken instruction or question. Was it a parting benediction or a direction for slipping a rival into a ditch—which ?

All mounted and out of the paddock at last, they rode down to the start—a field of nine. The chill of adventure that precedes heated endeavour on them now. Horses were reaching at their bits, pulling and boring and rushing that bank on the way to the start with various mistakes and more various recoveries.

Much joking with the starter and two false starts before they are off. A wicked pace they rode into that first fence—a narrow bank too, but all got safely over it. The next was a bit too high to make fun of, and here a couple took it. A loose horse galloped on with the leaders who were taking a strong pull now, for here they crossed a road and turned right-handed. We lost them while they jumped two fences. Then they came into view again, galloping on over two stone walls in succession. A field of plough with an upstanding bank out of it—here's where some one is due for a fall ! Yes, a tiring horse hits it good and proper ; up goes his tail, and he's end-over-tip into the next field. Four fences on the down-hill now, and the five left in the race are riding pretty venomously at them. Again we lose them behind a little wood of larch.

Micky is no longer to be seen, fallen or pulled up somewhere out of sight. There's a chestnut horse going up into the lead now and the crowd roars enthusiasm for his jockey as they lead over the last fence. And a brute it is, too, with a boggy take-off and the landing sloping towards it, so that each horse seems to go right into the ground as he lands.

Short right-handed they turn now and race for an iniquitously narrow gap with stout stone pillars on either side of it. Then a long up-hill run in (the two hunt servants keeping the

RIDING PRETTY VENOMOUSLY.

course have all they can do to prevent the crowd from surging in endless waves across it). A great finish between the favourite and a little pony of a roan mare. But the mare swerved under the whip, and the chestnut horse's jockey sat still and kept hold of his horse's head—to win by half a length amidst uproarious enthusiasm.

Salmon sandwiches and a thermos of soup laced strong with sherry-wine, and down to the last fence again to watch them over it. There we saw an incident fraught with drama— Success, Mishap, Effort, Failure, Victory, as closely mingled as they ever are in Life or in Racing ! It happened like this : a field in advance of the rest of the horses a young lad, mad with excitement, came charging into the last fence. Not a doubt about it he had the race won, and, to judge by the silence of the spectators at this ultimate obstacle, his victory would be one of those too frequent good things which nobody is on. No man may say how many times in the course of the race this jockey had missed a flag—these things *will* happen out in the country—but when at this distressingly public moment he went the wrong side of a red flag there was nothing for it but to pull up and leap the fence back and back again. Even so, all might have yet been well had the gallant little horse not pecked on landing so badly that his jockey went out somewhere between his ears—a desperate moment and a desperate struggle. Any one of the spectators standing by could have caught him and shoved him back into the saddle, but not one of them moved. They were on the favourite to a man and no false feelings of sportsmanlike sentiment were going to overcome their better judgment. But he got back, that game young lad, and I like to remember how, adhering by faith and suction in place of the usual aids, he won his race, defeating the well-backed favourite by half a length. A proper fall we

THEY WERE ON THE FAVOURITE TO A MAN.

THE LOVELY FROM A FASHIONABLE COUNTRY.

saw, too, and joined the necrophilian crowd that surged about the jockey as he struggled to his feet, and fell again, to lie horridly still. I see that tall Priest of God laying about him in the crowd with a useful ash plant as he cleared a way for the doctor. So effective and right he was in his treatment of us idle gapers.

The ladies' race was the next event on the card and it looked a soft thing for the Lovely from a fashionable country whose mount had travelled to the course in a motor horse-box and who had arrived herself—complete with dashing swain— in a powerful, pale blue motor-car.

Quite aside from the fact that she was a lovely girl and had ridden the winners of several point-to-points this season, the little horse she owned and rode looked fit and well. On looks there was no doubt either of them could give a couple of stone to any one of the local Amazons and honest hunters upon which they were about to venture their persons over three miles of a dirty course. Good hunters and great jumpers, no doubt, at their own pace, but it looked rather as if they might be carried off their feet to-day.

The jockeys, gallant girls, were very variously turned out for the contest. I especially liked the Queen of the Bogs who wore her Russian boots and her sporting great-aunt's bowler hat with a wide band of black elastic beneath her chin. She was in a class by herself for, to be quite fair, most of the others were tidily enough attired in seventeen-and-sixpence worth of pathetically new high-necked pullover and their hunting breeches and boots.

There was a big field of them, set, each one, to ride a jealous race. Nine hardy lasses came under the starter's orders, and when the flag fell, went off as though all were lost. The danger looked grave for every one, but the lovely visitor went

THE QUEEN OF THE BOGS.

on and kept out of all trouble and interference. The little horse jumped like a stag and could obviously gallop away from the lot of them.

But these soft things come undone now and then in the strangest fashion, and to-day, after sucessfully negotiating the last obstacle on a barbarous course, Miss Stranger was riding gracefully up the straight to win, it seemed, as she liked. When, into the fence, as if it were not there, came the Queen of the Bogs to ride such a thrilling finish on her rateen of a pony against that possibly Punchestown horse as one may not often see.

The Sporting Piece from strange parts had stopped riding and indeed was properly caught napping. She yielded even the inside to the aboriginal who came from nowhere to win by half a length among scenes of intense local enthusiasm.

Were the tears very near the poor sweet's eyes as she congratulated the winner in the weigh-tent? I am not sure that they were so far off, but she was a generous Lovely and took her defeat nobly. Especially as rumour said she had had a packet on her horse.

And then that Farmers' Race, its start delayed a good twenty minutes while search was made through cars and crowds and down the course for an M.F.H., whose certificate for fair and regular hunting of an entry the horse's owner had neglected till thus late to procure.

But at last they were all under the starter's order. I had my eye—and a pound, too—on Micky, who rode again that sporting old horse, and I hoped he had benefited by his earlier school. He had. He jumped that first fence in grand style. Nor did Micky ever join the crowd that clouted and fell in gaps. He was right. The dangers of the fences were lesser dangers than those of the shorter course. I saw three who raced for a gap all take a pull at the last and fatal moment and meet in a treble murderous fall. No. Micky rode a great race and a strong finish. I shared fully in the enthusiasm of his parent who gathered him into a vast, red-bearded embrace, kissing him twice and again with tears as he dismounted to weigh in. . . .

What, then, my dismay when I sought my bookmaker to hear that sinister word " Objection " on all sides resounding !

" Arrah, God ! What objection ? " One who, like myself, had backed Mr. Micky Fenessey's Flying Boy, inquired of a friend in the crowd : " Isn't that horse well qualified to run and did Micky go nigh or next one in the race could object him ? "

Within the tent the objection pursued its course. From a vortex of abusive denunciation and denial the stewards at last gathered the gist of the matter.

" Well," said the objector in final statement, " this horse is not qualified to run in any farmers' race."

" And on what grounds do you object to him ? "

" 'Tis not the horse I object, 'tis the owner."

" And on what grounds "—a patient steward asked again, silencing Micky's angry interruption—" do you object to the owner ? "

" Tell me who is Micky Fenessey to call himself a farmer ? "

" Why wouldn't I ? " said Micky belligerently, " and I with eighteen store cattle on me place ? "

" Ye have, maybe," replied the objector. He paused a weighty moment before delivering his broadside : " But haven't ye a lake wid a *shwan* on it ? "

Strange as it may appear, however, this objection was over-ruled by the stewards, who did not hold that the possession of ornamental water necessarily precluded the occupation of farming.

"AND YE'LL BE SAY-SICK WID LEPPING."

GOT HIM BATE.

"BUT HAVEN'T YE A LAKE WID A *Shwan* ON IT?"

" Winner all right," came through.

I gathered in my winnings and sought the car. The day's racing was over. Ah, but such a day ! Again I see the gorse burning narrowly on every fence ; the transient arch of a gull's wings against the mountains ; and again the speed and the effort of this day's horse-racing entrances me beyond excitement.

CHAPTER III

THE ATHENRY COUNTRY

MUCH talk there was in the club in Peshawar over the finest view in Europe or in Asia. Some said it was in the County Meath. Others saw it with the Braunston Vale spread out below them. Some would have it nearer at hand and swore they found no view or moment equal to those when—with the sun coming up beyond the green of the Peshawar Vale, and the Khyber hills rose-pink in the distance —hounds are running on over a country of banks and drains, a sure point of four miles in the making and never a sign of wire or cry of " Ware Wheat."

But my friend, Martin O'Hara, from the banks of the Shannon would have none of them. He maintained that the Athenry country of the Blazers could give the lot a stone and a beating. And, which was more to the point, if any of us cared to pay him a visit there when, in 1931, he settled down on his ancestral acres, we might have our fill then of galloping and jumping—lepping, though, he had it.

He was as good as his word too, and after Christmas of that

year all was in order for my day with the Blazers. I was to cross from Holyhead to Dublin ; apparel myself for the chase on the boat ; catch the Limerick express (which leaves Dublin at seven o'clock) and he would meet me at Cloughjordan Junction.

But between plan, departure and arrival there were moments when I wished most bitterly that I had never embarked my person upon this adventure. When the *Hibernia* reeled and shuddered under the buffetings of the year's worst gale—or so a comforting steward described it as he ministered. When I turned out on Kingstown Pier in the January morning, bleak and black. When, my boots and breeches marking me out as a possible carrier of foot and mouth, I was politely but firmly conducted to a small room and then fumigated— to come out looking like an advanced case of yellow jaundice and longing for a kind, quick death. But the guard of the train put me in a first-class carriage in spite of my third-class ticket. He was a good kind man. He understood much. Later a grimy girl brought me a cup of tea—smoky but hot.

" I'm sorry," said she, " for the delay bringing it, but meself and the guard was stuck under the stove this half-hour and we couldn't knock a spark from it—'tis a cross old yoke to light, God knows——" A good-humoured girl and a guard whose devotion to duty, official and otherwise, must not go unpraised.

Martin met me at Cloughjordan—a cheerful sportsman is he. His light, bright blue eye sees a great deal that he never says, for he talks more and gives away less than most people I know. The sheepskin collar of his brown leather coat was turned up cowl-like about his ruddy face, and its belt was tightly drawn around his stubby body. He is a hard worker and a brilliant man to hounds, riding a hunt with that quiet and immediate decision that belongs to the elect.

His house, to which we drove now, was old and untidy, and rambled up the east bank of the Shannon with a beautiful sweep of grass before it down to the river and the Portumma bridge. Martin told me that during the " troubles " the bridge was held by the Free Staters, and the *Fianna Fail* occupied a spinney in the demesne—the house was in a direct line of fire between it and the blockhouse on the bridge, his lawn and vegetable garden the No Man's Land. Was anybody hit ? I asked, but—bless you—no ; we were always warned before the opening of a bombardment.

I had a drink then and got ready for the road. The car, with Daphne (his wife), two children and another girl seemed fairly crowded, so I volunteered to go with Martin in the front seat of the horse-box—a home-made affair this, a bathing-machine-like body set upon an old Chevrolet lorry chassis. We were taking two horses in it ; three had been sent on, two of these would travel home in the box and the two we were taking on their flat feet—sound management !

The horses went into the box like two big dogs, the tail-board was secured and off we went. The conveyance seemed to me a bit top heavy, we hugged the centre of the road and at every turn we luffed a bit and got down into low gear. Martin told me that he and Daphne and the young were going to use it as a caravan in the summer months.

The country we drove through was a rolling sea of wonderful grass, but fenced so close with stone walls that from the middle distance to the horizon the colour was brown, changing towards blue. For here the retiring seas of the Atlantic have left upon the land a strata of water-worn stones over which as the land came up this turfy grass has formed. The early Irish agriculturist delved down a foot or so for his fencing material, and now all the stones have been rooted from the land and piled up in four-foot walls round three and four-acre fields. As there are no gates (a hole is knocked in the wall and built up again as the cattle are driven in), the biggest glutton for lepping can have his stomach full of it here.

Martin told me these and other things as we drove along —stories of the local gentry, tales of hunts and horse deals. But one scrap of local history has remained in my mind and set fancy many times alight since then. It was a tale of an old house he showed me, a house standing tall and grey in its woods ; beauty about it and sorrow, and an inviolable dignity. Here, he said, the Ralphe family have lived since bow-and-arrow days. For, by the grace of God, it had not been handed over to one of Cromwell's colonels. The Sir Jocelyn Ralphe of those days had been overbold for the dangerous times, so bold indeed that one of Oliver's colonels was sent down to Galway to take over the estate. Arriving one fine morning, he rode up to the hall steps and demanded Sir Jocelyn's immediate presence.

Old and bold in his brocaded dressing-gown, Sir Jocelyn descended his steps to speak with this rude disturber of his morning's rest ; and as Cromwell's soldier bent forward in his saddle to show him the documents of his authority, this cunning old sir whipped out his sword from the folds of his dressing-gown and with a back-handed upper-cut sliced off his head. Away galloped the horse with the headless carcass flopping about in the saddle, for the high cantle of these days would keep even a lifeless man firmly in the plate.

And what followed ? I wondered. Surely a sorry retribution ? But no ; Cromwell forgot for once to visit his wrath and the family heard no more of the matter until, a few years ago, some lads cutting turf in the bog uncovered the skeletons of a horse and a headless man, and so established as history that savage legend of the family.

And now we saw before us a string of horses quietly jogging along the soft side of the road, three chestnuts bringing up the rear. A groom led two and a slip of a girl rode the third. The three chestnuts, Martin told me, were his, and the slip of a girl his children's governess—very obliging lass—would turn her hand to anything, from teaching the youngsters to doing second horsewoman. As we drew near, down came the governess's horse, and Martin, cursing freely, pulled up the van and jumped out to ascertain the extent of the damage to his horse. The only damage, however, had been sustained by the obliging girl, whose knee was bleeding profusely through a large hole in her jhodpores. Nobody wasted much sympathy on her, however, and we set about unloading the horses.

Hounds were meeting at a house two miles distant, but a less convenient place for unloading than our present halt, as its more aristocratic park did not provide the plenitude of loose stones with which the tail-board of the van must be scotched up before it might safely bear a horse's weight. So we plucked stones from the walls—the governess limping but uncomplaining. The horses were backed out and we replaced the stones in the wall.

The next thing being to get to the meet, Martin suggested that I should ride on with Johnny, the groom, while he followed with the horse-box and the lame governess.

But first he introduced me to my horse. " A proper stag over the walls," said he; " he's won nine point-to-points— so if we have a hunt you'll be in the front row of the stalls. Oh, damn," he said, " if I haven't come out without

my spurs. Lend me yours like a good man—you won't
want 'em on Jimmy-the-One—the yoke I'm riding is a bit
of a slug."

No. I did not think I should want them on Jimmy-the-One.
If ever I saw a keen-looking horse here he was, this little blood-
like chestnut. A white blaze he had and four white stockings—
light of his middle perhaps, but grand strong quarters and
hocks on the ground—absolutely on the ground. I hoped I
might make good use of him, but rather thought it might be
the other way about.

However, I climbed up and caught hold of the reins of
Daphne's old horse, Harlequin—a real old-fashioned type of
confidential cut-and-come-again hunter—and followed Johnny
the groom, leading two and riding one, down the narrow
stone-walled road.

The horses were all on their toes, particularly my Jimmy,
and it was with well-founded trepidation that I observed a
young lad carting stones in the road before us, a gay-looking
old ex-hunter in the shafts of his cart. Nor were my fears
ill-founded, for the day's greetings were hardly over, and the
shattering roar with which a load of stones was loosed forth
upon the roadside survived with but a minor exhibition of
nerves by our horses when, with a clatter and a rattle and a
great whoa-whoa-whoa-ing, the old hunter under the cart
came merrily bucketing down the road to join us, the lad
running behind at the best pace he could compass. Johnny
started his three horses into a canter to ease the shock of
impact and shouted to me to follow, which I did. Jimmy-the-
One, thinking this a good opportunity to get going, hotted
me up nicely trying to hold both him and Harlequin. Dreadful
things over-fresh horses are. A tree sticking out at a bend in
the road saved the situation before matters quite escaped from

He had held the rank of Brigadier in the Sinn Fein Army.

my control by getting between the near wheel and the body of the cart, thus bringing the runaway up with a round turn and giving the lad a chance to get up to it and catch hold of the reins.

At the meet the crowd was a smarter one than is often seen in Ireland. The Master and hunt servants were beautifully mounted. There were two or three hardy lasses, two or three good-looking girls, half a dozen soldiers home on leave, and a good showing of the local gentry and farmers. Of the last breed one particularly foxy-looking lad I observed riding a four-year-old blood sort of horse and wearing a much-patched pair of field boots, breeches and coat to suit and a bowler hat which had had all the stiffening crashed out of it long ago, and a face that weather and whisky had matured to a ripe magenta. Martin told me that he had held the rank of brigadier in the Sinn Fein army and it was thanks to him and his sporting tastes that the local fox-hunters' houses had remained un-burnt in those troublous times. Then there was the doctor—no hunt complete without its sporting doctor—on a short-tailed dun Connemara pony with a black stripe down its back (he went like a bird all through the hunt that followed), and a youth whose paper-thin racing boots stopped two inches short of his breeches. These and many more, but hounds moved off before I could observe them more intimately, and I had little attention to spare from Jimmy-the-One, for I had by now arrived at the disturbing conclusion that I was distinctly and definitely over-horsed. And this, before hounds had even found, was not a very comforting thought. But when their voices crashed through the grove of wood and laurel they were drawing and a halloa beyond proclaimed their fox was on, I abandoned all craven tremors and knew again the fever of the chase that is near to tears as we galloped down a ride in

A Stag of a Horse.

the woods, through the demesne gates, across the road, and popped over the wall into a field, beyond which hounds were driving along on a good scent.

Jimmy landed, it seemed, into the middle of the field, gave a couple of fly-bucks just to hearten me, and long before I had time to make up my mind as to which was the softest spot in the oncoming wall, we were up to it and over. No doubt a stag of a horse. And with the conviction that it was going to take me all my time to hold him between the obstacles I knew too why Martin had borrowed my spurs.

Walls and more walls! Dammit, there were more walls than fields—" and ye'll be say-sick wid lepping——" A field ahead was the Master, his two whippers-in galloping stride for stride with him on either hand and his hounds running on nicely just a field in front of him. They swung left-handed from us, crossing a road, and as we jumped in and out of it we could see them clustered round a spot in the middle of a field which turned out to be a drain covered over with slabs of flat stone. The second horseman with terrier appearing at this moment, a little red bitch about as big as a large ferret was put in—her hackles up and her long-docked tail wriggling, just like a ferret. It was while I was watching the evicting operation that a friendly voice informed me that my bridle was off. I dismounted at speed and clasped Jimmy-the-One round the neck, while Martin put matters right with a mild cursing of that fool Johnny who had obviously put the big horse's bridle on the little horse.

Before long the mining operations were abandoned and the Master, deciding to leave Charles in undisputed possession of a drain that obviously maintained its functions below several hundred acres of pasture, moved off to draw the Laragh bog.

In the next twenty minutes I wished many times that the draw had been close at hand ; or that the way thither had been gated ; or that we might have approached by lane or road. Jumping stone walls from a stand and maintaining that execrable pace, a hound jog, over the fields between them was a mode of progression through a country to which Jimmy-the-One was temperamentally unsuited. Matters developed into a bit of contest between us as to whether our progression should be in the middle of the pack or at a proper and respectful distance therefrom. A herd of young cattle, mad for joining the chase at the one possible point of egress from a field, proved the consummation of my difficulties. I cracked my whip at them, which was more than Jimmy-the-One, brought up on a " plant " (ash, well understood) and unused to a whip thong, could stomach. He made an eel-like sideways plunge away from it and I was gone. However, I managed to keep hold of the reins and climbed back into the plate again, shaken and frightened but, I thought, unhurt.

Laragh—a big bog, cold and deceitful. Pale reeds and rushes to hold a fox and pools of still black water, cold skies told again in their stillness. A plantation at one end and one way only through the hazards of bog holes. *Not* a good place to see hounds go away on the far side from us, as we did. No cutting across that desolate morass was possible. We galloped along parallel with them, and by the greatest good luck they turned right-handed to us as they left the bog. So we cut in and sat down to ride what looked likely to prove a stern chase.

Right-handed again out of a road and over an awe-inspiring stone wall, and we are indeed in the front row of the stalls. It was then that the Master spoke a few firm words. But as for taking a pull on Jimmy it was as much as I could do to prevent him going stride for stride with the foremost hounds. And what a feel he gave me as he rocketed over the walls and laid himself down to gallop over those fields with the going like a carpet and never a sign of wire to quench our ardour. And what a grand sight—twenty or thirty red and black coats bobbing up and down as they popped over the walls of the small enclosures, no sooner settled down in the plate than the prospect of the next was near.

Twenty-five minutes hounds ran on without a check and when they threw up, where their fox had run through a flock of sheep, the Master's forward cast speedily put matters right again.

They were pointing now towards the woods of a demesne. We crossed a road, jumping into and out of it from a stand ; galloped across a wider field than any we had met and then saw hounds leaping at the face of the ugliest obstacle yet encountered —a demesne sunk fence faced up with stones—not very pretty. However, somehow we all got over it.

After this the going became none so pleasant—rabbit holes, and deep cart tracks through a virgin forest of Portugal laurel. I was getting very blown and almost yearning for a cessation of some kind, but Jimmy was more than ever keen for the chase. His bright chestnut was no longer that hue but a shiny liver colour ; my reins were wet and slippery. It took me all my time to keep at a moderately respectful distance from the Master. I followed him over a wall and into a still thicker plantation of laurel and cannoned into his horse's quarters as he turned sharp after he landed, well meriting my cursing. I think I was asked to refrain from following him about like a sucking lamb.

Not a doubt but Jimmy was in charge now, even the one side of him which was all I had ever presumed to ride I could now

A DASH GOOD RIDDANCE TO BOTH.

no longer dispute. But, hounds running over an open country once more, I could for the moment sit there and leave him in charge. Still, I was not very happy—to be entirely over-horsed is one of the worst sensations I know. Jumping through a gap in a wall, I received a fearful smack on my worst corn from a stone, and groaned aloud in anguish. Calamities heaped themselves upon me thick and fast after this. Jimmy made a slight mistake in landing over a wall, I made a worse one and lost an iron, which I did not recover for some time as it flew up behind me, and I sat on the leather. Then a young horse, clipped trace high and filled with disgusting youthful enthusiasm, leaped out of its field and attached itself with dreadful perseverance to Jimmy-the-One.

Remembering my experience with the cattle, I dared make no use of my whip, nor had I any choice save to endure. My final mishap came at an outsize in walls beyond which was a tarred road. Jimmy and I and the loose horse jumped it in a bunch, and the latter gave me a savage clout, I'll swear. However that may be, I left the saddle very light and airy, and landed on my back on the grass edge of the road. I gathered myself up to see my horse and his young attendant jump the wall out of the road and go a good gallop across the field towards the next obstacle.

.   .   .   .   .   .

The Irish side-car and its perils are, or were, too widely known to require description, so when one of this nearly defunct species came swaying and rattling—a curious combination of motions—down the road and halted beside me I climbed upon it in an obedient trance, for I was very shaken by all this, and surrendered the guidance of my immediate procedure to the enthusiastic old gentleman who drove it. It was, I decided, as we split off down the road at a hand canter,

Me two feet in a Bog.

THE ONE TO KEEP IN THE CORNER OF YOUR EYE.

a form of road-hunting in which the dangers of the chase were
not entirely obliterated. For a mile at least we rocked and
bounced savagely, and I, clinging to everything within reach,
told of my hunt and my misadventure, and he heard me with
a good half of his attention, the rest being given to our safe
conduction and to the country on either side of the road.

" *Yonder* they go ! " he exclaimed at last with unaffected
conventionality and pointed with his coachman's whip to
where I could see the hounds casting themselves in a field,
unattended for the moment by any horseman. " It's for the
woods beyond he'll make," said my driver, " and the dogs
may say good-night to him there."

Just then the field came into sight—four of them all told
—and among them my horse, bestridden by a country lad
grinning half-way round his head, the peak of his cap reversed,
and his trousers tucked inside his socks, he was obviously
determined to see the end of this heaven-sent hunt. Had it
lain with me to prolong his brief ecstasy I must confess I
would have done so very gladly. But my friend of the side-car
took a more correct view of the matter. With a yell of mingled
wrath and command he summoned the youth to the roadside.
Nor did he drive on until I had climbed once more into the
saddle. And this, having bestowed half a crown on Jimmy's
capturer, I unwillingly proceeded to do. My enthusiasm for
the chase dead now within me, I heard hounds open as they
hit off the line again. The moment had arrived for me at
which the pleasures of fox-hunting turn into the nature of a
grim contest. However, dogged in my mind to make the best
of the best horse I was ever likely to ride, I had turned him
round to leap out of the road when, music to my ear indeed,
I heard Martin's voice as he and his wife came riding down
the road towards me. I need hardly say that I applauded his

POINT AND TIME AND DANGERS PAST.

notion that the horses had done about enough and that, in view of our long ride back to the horse-box, we might without dishonour leave things to the gentlemen with second horses.

" For," said Martin, his eye directed onwards from the hounds towards the sudden darkness of that near wood, " they won't be out of those dreary woodlands till six o'clock to-night."

So in my mind I see that moment again, clear as glass ; the grey walls, the grey fields, the grey sky. And I hear the hounds' voices, abiding and lovely on the air, now that the strife to be with them for me is over. I see their huntsman and one servant still taking the shortest way over the country, their distant effort apart from us now in the gentleness suddenly come upon us. To write the tale of a hunt well and truly requires that its end should be in the death of a fox, but I shall never know how this notable chase concluded. Not thus, I think. Nor can I even say whether or how he was accounted for. I left while hounds were still hunting their fox and while better men than I lived with them still. In place of the hot achievement of completing this hunt I saw this romantical moment, and I may forever hold it mine.

Back along the roads we went quietly jogging and walking, the promise of tea before us, for we would call in at a friend's house and give the horses a drink on our way back to the box, the sweet interminable discussion of Point and Time and Dangers Past our present pleasure.

At an old Georgian house we dismounted from our horses, leading them round its wide-spread wings to the quiet stir of the stable-yard, and presently sitting down to the best of all teas, eggs and bacon and potato cakes, preceded by whisky of a peculiar excellence ; an old liqueur brand extinct now, known as " Tabby-toes." I cannot easily forget it. And through its mellowing warmth I can see again the strong and graceful lines of all the Chippendale and Sheraton furniture with which the dining-room was crowded. The serpentine front of a grimy and unpolished sideboard fills me now with delight, and I grieve to have forgotten the various series of prints which hunt upon the walls.

In an easy languor we left that house at last and climbed once more on to our horses (the third horse would stay out the night, he was so far from his own country), and rode forth along the ribbon-straight avenue into a dusk the colour of blackberries and tarnished silver, and so on for eight miles of a hack back to the horse-box. Tired now past any pleasant languor, we saw our horses walk quietly in, and disposed ourselves in that friendly silence which endured between us for the long drive home.

.   .   .   .   .   .

So ended a day in the Athenry country. But the night was before us still. Willingly would I have parted with the half of all that I had might I have retired to my bed at half-past nine that same evening.

But it was not to be. The men and women of County Galway are a tough and enduring breed. They ride incredible hunts by day and by night they are not defeated. They frivol with tireless enthusiasm.

Besides, this was the night of the Hunt Ball of a neighbouring county. No evening to avoid out of gaiety. At such a time we must be bright or die. When I discovered—crowning adversity on a hunting day—that my bath water was cold, on the whole I rather wished I might die. But such a quiet and humane end was not for me. Surviving the semi-cold and shallow bath (we had been informed by James, the house-boy, that the big

end of the pump had died on it, and would we go aisy wid
the water) and the dreadful exhaustion of attiring my body
for the party, I began to find myself infected with the general
enthusiasm. Nor while the night lasted did I loose my
form.

To begin with, Martin's drink was of the very soundest.
And at the end of dinner he produced an old brandy of a
beauty and excellence that I love to remember. It was after
this, I think, that the evening began to go with what one might
vulgarly describe as a swing.

We proceeded at high speed to the dance, which was held
in a private house, as all good balls should be, and there we
rioted untiringly hour after hour. There is a quality about
such a gathering in Ireland which I think I have not known
elsewhere. The veriest stranger is included in the silliest joke
or unkindest scandal and is for the moment allowed to belong
to the life of the country. This admittance is as pleasant as it
is no doubt unreal. I did enjoy myself so much. And when—
crowning incident of the evening—the electric light failed
completely, I even had a shrewd idea as to Who had cut the
cable and Why, and Whose cousin was involved, and What
his Wife had said, and Why Did the Lovely? Oh, she was
a lovely, gay creature too. And so full of her jokes. Did she
not put a *méringue* down his Wife's back in the dark? But
that was all because (mounted on a horse with very large
feet) his Wife had really done her damnedest to jump on the
Lovely's face when the Lovely had taken a crashing fall last
Thursday week. . . . And so on through the night things
were kept going with drink and laughter, and much dancing.
I shudder to think of the hour at which the generous band
packed up and the last beer and bones was eaten.

I was not meant for such late nights. Perhaps I am of a

softer breed than these Athenryites. I cannot quite stay the course with them. And, in any case, I would like to say that there must be a law made forbidding people to upset their motor-cars at six o'clock on a January morning. At such a time and after such a night one feels one's age, and one's folly, and the cold with an intensity not far off tears—if it was not so near to laughter.

CHAPTER IV

A SLANEY FISH

MUCH about the season when Stinkin' Violets blow and the miserable bunch-clod raises its diminished head, there is a certain germ that flies abroad. More virulent than any town-bred streptococcus, the " fishing-fever " germ fills us with a restless eagerness for the sound and sight of running water, and all the unfathomable charm of vain endeavour that only his victims know.

Irish salmon-fishing has a flavour of its own in the same subtle way that all sport in Ireland differs from English fare.

In March the smoke of heather burning makes lavender streaks across the darker purple of the mountains. In April the nearer hills are soaked in the musky-sweet bloom of gorse. In May, before the trees are darkened by the gad-fly heat of summer, salmon there are in plenty. But rivers now are running fine and skill is needed to bring success to the angler. Low water calls for low cunning. Now the gently-wafted shrimp takes the place of flashing Devon; flies are small and gut-links perilously fine.

A FISHERMAN STANDS CLOSE TO THE WATER'S EDGE.

Peter Beckford bluntly declared that he considered fishing a dull amusement, and many there are that share his views. Yet hunting and fishing are not so very far apart. It is interesting in this connection to see how many Masters of Hounds are keen fishers. There is the same necessity for searching out the ways and probing the secrets of things whose speech is not in words.

One does not need to be a fisherman to join that happy band of idlers lounging over the parapet of a grey stone bridge,

whose fine arches precariously straddle a salmon river somewhere in Ireland. Above the bridge a flat, its surface dancing
in the sun and breeze, extends to the next curve a few hundred
yards above. Under the arches the river rushes indignant at
its man-made yoke. The next two hundred yards make a
perfect low-water stand. At the head of the stream a fisherman
stands close to the water's edge, motionless and intent. His
battered clothes mingle with the background of grey stone
and brown earth. He is holding a little fourteen-foot rod
which he handles with an effortless swing. He seems to persuade
the line off the water and to guide rather than impel it on its
return journey.

It is Monday; the nets have been off over the week-end,
so the fisher is more than ordinarily expectant. Grease is on
his line and desire in his heart.

" The lads is after tellin' me they seen one lep there last
night, surely as big as a bullock, sir."

Larry, the ghillie, speaks. A ragged person with a
filthy pipe which he sucks energetically although no smoke
appears.

The little partridge-hackled March Brown goes busily on
its way, darting, chasing, twisting, hovering, searching the
river in a wide sweep as each eddy plucks the floating line.
No dazzling parti-coloured figment of the fly-dresser's imagina-
tion this, its body a few turns of hare's fur ribbed with finest
gold twist, and two strips of hen-pheasant tail for wing. Never
anything but skimpy, it has been so chewed and mauled by
fish that, could we but see it, it would seem more like a bit of
bark or twig than a salmon-fly.

The cast is fished out to the very end; then a careful step,
the line gathered up, and with a graceful ripple of old-seasoned
greenheart the fly goes skimming on another search. One step

A Whale of a Fish.

more and the fisherman's foot will almost touch a certain white stone, now half-submerged. This stone marks the " taking place." It means that his fly will pass through an eddy which reveals the presence of a large stone. Behind this rock the river has collected a strip of silvery river sand. Here fresh-run fish find at the same time shelter and a place where they can rub off the sea-lice which cling to them full thirty-six hours after they have left the sea. When conditions are right this spot is " stiff with fish."

Another step. Now or never. The cast is made, with an upstream " mend " to obviate all danger of a drag. The fly hangs for a second in the eddy and then goes, it seems un-willingly, upon its way. Suddenly a big puddle appears in the water, a head is seen, then, a long way from it, just the indication of a tail. Surely a whale of a fish ! He turns back for his lie. As he turns the line drags and sinks.

Now is the time.

Now, and not before, the rod is raised. Almost as exciting as viewing a fox away. The thrill, the period of anguished inactivity, ere the reel screams its " Gone Away."

The fish makes a frenzied race in a wide circle round the pool, a moment's pause, then he is off downstream like a tiger ; straight for the sea it seems. Nothing can stop him, least of all a fine grilse cast. The fisher follows hot-foot, striving to recover line but beaten all the way by the fish.

Larry finds his voice at last. " Don't let him down near the bridge, sir, or he'll surely break all ! "

The fish stops just in time. He has taken out most of the backing on the reel, and is a good sixty yards below where he was hooked.

" He's a grand fish, Larry—must be near thirty pound."

" He surely is, sir, an' forty pound." Larry is always

an optimist in these matters. "I declare to God I thought he had us bet the first dart."

Thinking better now of his first mad rush, the fish suffers himself to be "led" slowly upstream, a matter of thirty yards. Then: "Look out, he's off again." A desperate effort this. Round and round he goes, the line zipping viciously through the water, then out he comes, a bar of flashing silver, in a mighty effort to shake the No. 7 from his jaw. A second time he jumps and still the cast is unsevered. A few minutes

LARRY BRANDISHING A FIVE-FOOT GAFF.

in which to recover from these lightning shocks and he is off downstream again. This time at a steady purposeful sort of pace, boring sideways to the pull so as to take full advantage of the stream. The fisher puts on every ounce of strain the cast will bear, but it is hopeless to say " No " to a thirty-pounder when he has made up his mind.

" Get in below him, Larry, or he's gone," screams the fisher. " Quick now ! "—as the half-reformed poacher seems unwilling to face the waters whose chill he has reason to dread. However, Larry and the fish make a concerted dive for the narrow channel guarded by the fatal " Pot Rock." *Salmo Salar* is forced, in the event, to yield to *Vis Major* in the shape of Larry brandishing a five-foot gaff ; he retreats in disorder upstream.

Now the crisis is past. Ten minutes steady pressure brings him lashing to the surface. Another five and he comes in to the bank. Larry's aim has been shaken by his unwelcome immersion and the first chance to gaff is missed.

" Damn you, Larry, what good are you ? " from the fisher in an agony of suspense.

" I didn't miss him, sir, he wheeled."

The next time the fish did not wheel. A splash, a grunt of satisfied accomplishment and a fresh-run thirty-pounder is kicking and flapping on the grass.

" Well, an' isn't he a darlin' ? " says Larry, aiming a few vicious blows to quiet the kicking. A murmur of satisfaction from the enraptured audience on the bridge, and—well, I ask you, wasn't it worth while, that little wait ? Is there a moment when the rapture of Achievement is more acutely personal than in the death of a fish ? A savage and necessary cunning of hand and eye, a measure of patient endurance are fulfilled. In such moments one forgives all Life's unkindness ; for them there is an imperishable gratitude and a thrill in remembering which too seldom survives Achievement.

CHAPTER V

"MORNING, Jim."

"'Tis a harsh day, yer honour, surely."

The first speaker is seated on the running-board of his car meditatively stuffing cartridges into a canvas-webbing belt, the while he surveys a wide purple and brown expanse of bog which flings its jagged two-mile breadth around, and as if to soothe, the angry slapping waters of a lough. The wind is half a gale from the north and west, laden with sleet, and the day as cold as is to be met with in Kerry, where snow is rare and hard frosts almost unknown.

Cold on his left hand the Atlantic beats in to shore, a grey sad coast this time of year, with little houses along it that turn their banks and seem to crouch into themselves against the day's unkindness. Forgotten the summer when their fuchsia hedges and hedges of Escalonia bloomed with a tropical luxuriance. Yes, and Arum lilies grew in such strange divorcement from weddings and funerals as to make them appear almost unseemly in this wild place. The foxgloves are better flowers here and their profusion is more exquisite. Nowhere are there such foxgloves as in Kerry. They grow upon every wall and stony bank, leaning their gay spires far up where they can grasp a roothold upon the grey screes of the mountain's feet—and in Kerry the mountains are never far from the sea. The turf bogs and the little loughs run from the sea and cut into the mountains, and the mountains' heights open and close again behind them. Somehow the small black Kerry cattle are the only fitting breed for these places, they are as active as deer and can leap fences like seasoned hunters or like the small grim mountain sheep that one sees disappear unharmed down drops of incalculable steepness.

But that is the Kingdom of Kerry in the summer weather when there is soft rain falling or sun and shadow changing on the mountain passes, and the Fisher goes about his business on lough and sea and river. This is not his hour. To-day a shooter sits, worn riding breeches, thick stockings and greasy hobnailed boots covering the lower limbs of him, while from his shoulders droops a loose-fitting, ragged tweed coat reserved for lonely expeditions in doubtful weather, such as this one bids fair to be.

The second belt, each cartridge in which carries one and an eighth ounces of No. 8 shot, is filled at last and buckled on, sandwiches and a dog-biscuit are stowed in a special pocket of the game bag, and with the suspicion of a whistle to Lob, the Labrador, the gun slips through a sagging gate which separates the lane from the scene of operations.

Snipe are peculiar birds in more ways than one. It is not that they are the only, or almost the only, kind of wildfowl which may not be shot without a game licence and so are a cut above their fellows. It is not just their fascinating way-wardness that endears them; their whickering, glancing,

THE INFORMERS.

"THE BIGGEST WALLS IN THE COUNTHRY WAS IN IT"

JIM.

dodging flight ; their call, so unlike any human sound—perhaps best compared to the sharp squelsh of water inside a boot. More than their mysterious appearances and dis-appearances, regulated by wind, season, temperature and the phases of the moon, their charm has to do with the wild lonely places where they are to be found. Brown withered tussocks stuck in soft, treacherous mud and grouped about little pools of peaty water. Flattened knolls of heather with bent-grass at its roots, and here and there dark-green gorse bushes nibbled smooth by goats or donkeys.

Those who shoot snipe regularly know that the bird has exceptional hearing upon which it relies, aided by its spear-like bill, to locate worms deep down in the mud. Thus it is that in still frosty weather the brushing of large boots against wet rushes, and occasional unavoidable splashing in shallow pools, will often-times prevent a gun from approaching, as the saying is, " within the bawl of an ass of them." To approach the bird down-wind would at first seem madness, but here again experience proves it otherwise. Snipe dislike flying down-wind. They will sit as close as they dare, and when they do rise will hang on the wind for a split second to give the gun a chance he must seize quickly or it is gone for ever.

The shooter, who knows all this and a great deal more, has just finished a whispered conversation with Jim, a casual poacher-sportsman who has " happened along " to watch operations and discuss prospects in the way that these gentlemen do. He has news of a nice lot of teal and some big duck and more besides, but this is to be a snipe day, and if the duck refuse to wait—well, bad luck to them.

Whatever his exact sphere of usefulness, Jim's company is always welcome. On days when snipe are not the prey his conversation lends a delight to the hours spent with him hard to surpass, and there is no doubt but that good conversation is one of the main delights of life.

Whether Jim is telling of a hare hunted in the mountains by the local trencher-fed pack of beagles. " Oo would love to hear de beagles," he would say in his lovely sing-song Kerry voice, " dere is no music like lishning to de beagles in de mountains." And he would go on to tell of his own dog, " was de reigning dog of all," and of a great hare hunt in which " he knewsed where she would go. He was in it before dem all. Before dem all he had her cot——" which sounds like a little luck and a lot of skirting. And he would tell too of the great drag hunts and the heavy bets made and taken on them. And of hounds long dead. Strains of blood lost. Or again, for he was a boatman on the lough and the favourite ghillie of many, there were tales of fish lost and caught and poached in divers manners, and of years, not like the present lean, mean years, when fish ran incredibly large and in equally incredible numbers, and fishers were endowed with skill unusual in the present day. Many tales he would tell, their points unemphasised by so much as a glance from light, quiet blue eyes. Nor did he ever seem to speak when one was not in the humour for his talking. He was as sensitive to a mood and took colour from it as easily, and in the same impalpable fashion in which his home-woven and dyed clothes seemed to borrow transient colour from every changing background of the countryside. Perfect ghillie and perfect companion.

A long beat down-wind parallel with the shores of the lough will bring the gun to the end of Bryan's bog by about one o'clock, when it will be time for rest and sandwiches. He loads and moves off, shifting carefully from foot to foot as one not wishing to be caught off his balance in the treacherous going.

Scape ! Scape !

Two snipe rise a good forty yards ahead and flicker away browner shadows upon brown rushes, hardly show-ing their tell-tale white breasts. The shooter half-raises his gun but refrains. A second later he has his reward, for a bird rises nicely a bare thirty yards to the left and heads for the lake. But ten yards and he collapses in the rushes, folding his wings bat-wise as he falls. It is always a pleasant omen to kill the first bird of the day.

Sic itur ambulando. By one o'clock much of the load has been transferred from cartridge-belt to game bag. A clump of gorse to break the wind and a dryish

patch of heather behind it speak eloquently of lunch. The bag is marshalled. Nine couple and (by inadvertence) a Jack do gladden the eye with their plump breasts, apple-green legs and olive beaks awry.

Lying there snugly sheltered from the beat-ing wind and looking out on heavy sky and hissing waves it seems ludicrous to look back or forwards to the hot, scented weeks of sum-mer. Dapping time ; the

season of green drake and daddy-longlegs, when great spotted trout and golden gillaroo raise leisured snouts to absorb their appointed food. A skilfully drifted boat will not put them down, nor will they be aware of danger till the bronzed Limerick bites firmly into tender flesh.

And those short rivers too, where salmon and sea trout almost jostle one another on their way up from sea to lough. Not at all times by any means it must be allowed, more often the angler has need of all his skill and all his patience, but these times are worth while for the sake of that grey morning when a fifteen-pound salmon takes one down the river and out to sea, where—the angler scrambling and slipping on wet seaweed—such a contest is waged that whatever its conclusion leaves one forever enthralled by its memory. There are other hours too, summer evenings when the voices of the sea and the river murmur together in a hushed contentment; when the mountains faint into dreaming skies and the sharp smell of turf smoke is the only reality left in the evening—that or the pearly turn of a gull's wings against the quiet seas. Even if

there is not much of a "take" on the trout these nights (and more often they are taking to the exclusion of all such realisation of an evening's beauty) one is stilled away from all the ills of life, all discontent becomes an impossibility of ingratitude and such things as the turning of a floating fuchsia flower in a dark curl of water, and the first star, pale as an old moon, have their own true value and importance.

But that coveted twenty couple is still to get, and chilled limbs and an empty pipe warn the shooter that it is time to start the long beat round the lake and back to the car. Now the wind is not so favourable and the snipe uneasy, and less numerous. It is half-past three and cartridges and light alike are nearly spent ere the waiting car is reached.

Fifteen and a half couple of snipe, one jack and a teal. Not altogether a bad day; there were two nice right-and-lefts and several satisfying long shots.

Dry Stockings and a Thermos are Comfort for a King.

GREY LAGS

CHAPTER VI

WHAT MATTER?

NOW that the Irish have set themselves and their country so entirely apart from sane consideration, there is—not surprisingly—a present fashion of looking towards Ireland and the Irish as towards a land and a people belonging to a past time. Ireland with her visionary wrongs and actual revenges, her taking of all and giving of nothing, has at long last succeeded in defeating even the liking of the majority of her English neighbours. No sane Irishman or woman—and there are just a few left—can quarrel with this view of the matter.

Forgotten for the dark present are all the jolly misconceptions about the Irish with their sticks called shillelaghs and hats called corbeens, their begorrahs and their mushas, and their stories about their pigs. That was all part of a misconceived idea of Ireland, and it was part of the same idea that every one who lived in Ireland owned good horses, kept open house and made almost a fetish of hospitality. Ireland was a country where one could pick up a high-class hunter, full of quality and up to weight, for the proverbial song, and where a future National horse might run unfit down the course at any local race meeting. A country where " one never knew." A country where the sublime and the ridiculous ran each other so close that no one could tell t'other from which, and in any case, the ridiculous always got the verdict, for the Irish are shy of the sublime.

That, broadly speaking, was the idea about Ireland which has now been superseded by a mental picture—if any one really bothers to think about the matter at all—of burnt and derelict country houses, of empty stables that were once full of good horses, of blank fox coverts, silent kennels and poached rivers.

Well, it is true that the fun in Ireland is not quite what it was, but where has it endured the same? And was Ireland really ever quite like these pre-war memories? Take, for instance—all fun and jokes apart for the moment—the buying and selling of horses. How many really high-class hunters—set these aside from brilliant performers and safe conveyances—were in the last twenty-five years picked up for fifty pounds or so?—the popular price of fiction. Comparatively speaking, very few. No doubt some sensational horses to be have gone for that song we are so often hearing about, but to balance the scales many others that have made fancy prices have turned out worse than unlucky.

It is not of these ephemeral past possibilities that we must think, but of the Ireland that really was, the Ireland that endures through present darkness and difficulties with the integral reasons for her charm unperished. And in twenty-five years Ireland, despite the dark times she has known, has changed less than most countries. Fox-hunting is the word most surely associated with Ireland, and while fox-hunting ceases not the best of God's gifts to the country endures. It would be sad indeed if in a land so made and fashioned for the chase the chase should come to an end, and it is surely something in the favour of Ireland's politicians that through the worst of the country's bad times fox-hunting would seem to have come through in its essence unscathed.

True, in the sense that the whole country is poorer, subscriptions lower and fields smaller, fox-hunting has suffered a sad change from the old gallant days when " military gintlemen " hunted in their hundreds and bought horses—good, bad and indifferent—all round them. No such customers now for the small farmer with a nice young horse to sell. . . . " A bit green yet, but well schooled—all he wants is plenty of hunting. But I'm telling ye it's more than hunting this horse should be at, when ye'll feel the bust he'll go below ye, ye'd partly think he could fly. And why wouldn't he win races ? Isn't he by a winner and out o' the dam o' winners ? " . . . That was where the young soldier, a pleasing vision of open light-weight races in various point-to-points within his grasp, and even—at the back of his mind—a faint hope : Punchestown, perhaps, would be tempted and would fall.

No. Those days of profitable horse-breeding are past now. But what endures is the true love of fox-hunting, a live spark in almost every Irishman of whatever class or kind. That enthusiasm for the chase which brings the young farmer out hunting on a horse he cannot now hope to sell inspires, too, the young lad who, moved to a nearly divine excitement by the cry of hounds and the magic notes on a huntsman's horn, will unyoke his horse from its ploughing and pursue while he may the hunt he loves.

Fox-hunting is in Ireland the thing that matters, the thing of first and last importance. The sorrows of life and the solemnities of death are not in comparison with its exigencies. Once I have seen a coffin and its funeral cortège stopped on their way to the grave because a fox had been viewed across the road before it. So proceedings were held up while a mourner was dispatched across country to give information to the huntsman whose hounds were at fault three fields from the road. Again, I have seen a hearse—empty this time—pause on the crest of a hill that its driver and some of his more favoured friends might view the point-to-point course with a ladies' race in progress below and around them. An excellent grand stand the hearse made too, no doubt, and one which groaned beneath their enthusiasm for a popular girl's popular win.

But it is not alone that peculiar bond in the love of hunting which exists in Ireland between those who do and don't, and shouldn't, but do hunt, which makes Ireland even now and to the present day so enthralling a country to hunt in. It is the country itself with its almost incredible beauty that captures so fiercely those who have ever hunted or loved hunting in Ireland. So many Irish counties are mountain-encircled plains that one may never quite turn one's back on distant height. Even though in the heat of the chase Beauty and Speed and Endeavour seem fused in a single rapture of excitement. There are other quieter hours in the course of a day's hunting when a deep joy in so much that is lovely translates a moment to something as near complete happiness as one may go. A hack out or home, or an unenterprising day on a green young horse. Then there is beauty in the lovely hills as a wild and fitting counterpart to the savage beauty of hounds hunting a fox; or hounds jogging back to kennel, tired and

FOX-HUNTING IS THE THING THAT MATTERS—THE SORROWS OF LIFE AND THE SOLEMNITIES
OF DEATH ARE NOT IN COMPARISON WITH ITS EXIGENCIES.

quiet after a long day, as the hills are quiet in the evening.

There are times in the earliest part of the season before the cub-hunting—hard work for huntsmen and slack times for hunting folk—is over, when the magic of hour and place weave an unforgettable spell. These mornings, when there is a mist so heavy as milk about the mountains' feet, and a little river appears suddenly dark and noisy through the fog, are dear and lonely times. In the unreal young day the hounds are like a fleet of ships in a blue sea of gorse and you hear their voices and the ghost-clear voice of a whipper-in : " Get-awi-huic. . . . Get-awi-huic. . . . Get-awi-huic. . . . Get-awi-on-to-'im on to 'im . . . on—on—on—on—on—on—on." . . . Impossible to recapture quite that moment or the importance to it of unseen mountains and wild, quiet distance interrupted only by a small and lonely farm with the bitter spell of its turf smoke not even yet about it. No small-holders' chicken-runs and back gardens yet, thank God. By the covert the water-pale jade of unripe hazel nuts enchants, and the near view of a little fox slipping across a close-grown ride quickens the spirit to a pitch of excitement as genuine to those who are lucky enough to know it as it is incomprehensible to those who are not.

And what a country for a young man hunting hounds—a difficult country to kill foxes in, yes—but a grand wild country in which to learn about doing it. Too many unofficial coverts perhaps, and stopping not always of the first order, but the blessed absence of a vast, ignorant and critical field is at least half the battle. Well, to be fair, it cannot be denied that Irish huntsmen have their criticisers (ignorant and otherwise), but such do not come out hunting in their hundreds, which is something to be thankful for.

Next, perhaps, to the lovely surroundings in which we hunt the fox in Ireland might be placed in order of enchantment the astonishing variety of obstacles which are to be encountered in almost any country in the course of almost any hunt—should we except the stone walls of Galway. The feeling of extreme uncertainty as to what obstacle he may next have occasion to leap fills the stranger to an Irish county with excitement certainly, sheer terror, perhaps, and (if he is lucky) with an unlimited, almost a holy, enthusiasm for the horse that has carried him with such unaided brilliancy throughout the day.

There is no doubt that the stranger to an Irish county must find it hard to distinguish at times between the jumpable and the unjumpable. There are, notably in the County Cork, some stone-faced banks to the top of which one would swear no horse could go, banks one would think they must hit half-way up, but they don't. Alarming as an obstacle of this sort may be, it is productive of considerably less grief than half the small and trappy fences one may encounter. One may go on a bit at the lower, narrower banks, chancing three out of four with safety, but the ditch on the landing side of the fourth puts one out of that hunt unless one is exceptionally well mounted. Beware the horse that chances his fences, giving you a grand feel and a few frights. One of these frights is going to be a dirty shock before the chase is over. Of course the ideal thing in any country is a horse that can gallop and jump, but in most Irish countries, that they should incontestably jump is the first essential. In fact, the horse that is going to jump an English country really well when he gets there is not the most con-fidential conveyance over banks that must quite often be jumped out of a bog and into a bog. And when you see one of those high, narrow ones, the top of it leaning towards you and the face of it eaten away, thank your stars if you are riding a common old hunter who has been at the game long enough to take such things seriously.

There are the elect and chosen few, it is true, who ride at speed over any country and in to almost any fence, from the end of the iron bedstead (which is popularly supposed to stop any gap in any small farm in Ireland and—strangely enough—often does) to the narrow bank with stones to the top of it, and very possibly the waters of a mountain torrent rattling beneath their canopy of briers on the farther side. All praise to them, they are lovely and gallant indeed, also, this is to be observed, it is only the rarer artists who are the incontestable exponents of this method of getting over the country, and they are generally mounted the very extra best.

You may see at the meet of many a pack of hounds in Ireland at least one exceptional and fatal-looking woman, superbly mounted and superbly well turned out, and you may think that she is the one to keep in the corner of your eye—and you a stranger in a strange land. But if hounds really run on you will be lucky or very brave if you succeed in keeping her there for long. These rare creatures can lose one and find one in a hunt without even seeming to hurry themselves. They know the very essence of the meaning of " quick off the mark," and, as has been said, they chance things in an incredible way, and if we can't always succeed in keeping them in the corner of an eye—luckily there is some kind providence which does that instead of us.

This sounds as though the girls cut out all the work, whicn is indeed far from the truth. The odd Miss Brilliancy just mentioned has many and many a sporting sister who tries, oh, so hard, with varying success—poor girl. Perhaps Love inspires her efforts sometimes, sometimes a sad itch of jealousy, but most often it must be admitted a genuine love of the chase. For, in Ireland, the majority of girls who hunt work really seriously for their hunting. It is a first importance with them and the sacrifices they make for it are real and earnest, nor do they count as sacrifice at all, because hunting matters so much to them. This is because hunting in Ireland is just possible for girls who would, in England, join the Badminton Club and put the Chase out of their heads as an impossibility anyhow. But these girls strive and struggle and scrape for their possible three days a fortnight. They clean—very in-differently—their one horse, and give up trips to London and new clothes, and many other things because of their passion, their really true passion for the Sport of Kings. And the years pass, the long dreary summer months and the swift delight of the winters, and the girls grow gently older until, at last, they find themselves the established spinsters of the Hunt, taking the places of Miss This and Miss That, who, with their fifteen-year-old habits wasp-waisted, curious hats and whips held upside down, told them off when they were girls, rode hunts as savagely as they were able and organised theatricals and hunt dances (ten shilling tickets and supper contributed), for the support of damage funds and the maintenance of fox-hunting in general.

Perhaps they are as good a type as any—these rather touching Irish spinsters—of the spirit that has made fox-hunting what fox-hunting is in Ireland. Their entire determination to enjoy one grand thing, and their pursuit of it in single-minded forget-fulness of other things that life has not given them, is rather typical of a country where, with horses unsaleable, overdrafts at the bank, and farming a dead loss, the general feeling is still one of hope for better times ; hope buoyed up by an indefeat-able optimism and gaiety, and " What matter ? "—the phrase

"WE CAN'T SELL THE HORSES, SO WE MAY AS WELL GET SOME FUN OUT OF THEM."

which best expresses that snatching of a happiness before it is gone wherein the Irish excel.

And aren't they right, these queer Irish people? If one does not hunt happily, leaving all dark anxiety behind one, surely it is better not to hunt at all. They know the secret of doing a thing gladly or letting it alone. " We can't sell the horses, so we may as well get some fun out of them. We'll all be broke together, so—what matter ? "

LEAVES FROM MY SKETCH BOOK

"Seen anything of hounds"
"What Hounds Sorr?"
"The Wexford Hounds"
"Shure now! didn't me mother come
from County Wexford"

WRECK AND RESCUE

I'll know another time. Yes, next time the lad with a cast in his eye, evil designs in his heart and ropes concealed upon his person appears from nowhere to indicate the one spot safe and jumpable in an otherwise impossible fence I'll think again before agreeing to that suggestion.

"Will I hearten him yer honour?"

When a good horse has said 'No'. A bad day to
get the wrong answer to a stupid question. a
grey evening with flakes of snow in the air – Not
the weather one would choose to slip back into (?) feet
of dirty grey water. No day to pursue one's horse
for any distance up the same ditch, or to
dispute the outrageous demands of the lad
with the ash-plant before ropes and rescue
are forth coming.

Or of the long hack with wet clothes,
wet cigarette, the nearest drink five
miles distant which followed.

"Catch a fox is it? If the dogs
can't he will"

THE HAARSE THRAINER

THE LADS FOR CATCHING HARDSHIP

THE GILLIE (an opportunist)

Now why wouldn't I he havin'
two drams and a split——

'twill be a while before he have
that one beshted'.

GOT IT WON

THE END
of a Perfect Day in East Galway